POSTCARDS · FROM ·

Great Britain

Helen Arnold

A ZOË BOOK

A ZOË BOOK

© 1995 Zoë Books Limited

Devised and produced by
Zoë Books Limited
15 Worthy Lane
Winchester
Hampshire SO23 7AB
England

First published in Great Britain in 1995 by
Zoë Books Limited
15 Worthy Lane
Winchester
Hampshire SO23 7AB

A record of the CIP data is available from the British Library.

ISBN 1 874488 52 5

Printed in Italy by Grafedit SpA
Editor: Kath Davies
Design: Jan Sterling, Sterling Associates
Map: Gecko Limited
Production: Grahame Griffiths

Photographic acknowledgments

The publishers wish to acknowledge, with thanks, the following photographic sources:

DDA Photo Library / Paul Juler 28; The Hutchison Library / Stephen Seque - title page; Robert Harding Picture Library 8; Impact Photos / Simon Shepheard 12; / Alain Le Garsmeur 16; / Tony Page 26; David Williams Picture Library - cover bl, 20; Zefa - cover tl & r, 6, 10, 14, 18, 22, 24.

The publishers have made every effort to trace the copyright holders, but if they have inadvertently overlooked any, they will be pleased to make the necessary arrangement

Contents

All the words that appear in **bold** are explained in the Glossary on page 30.

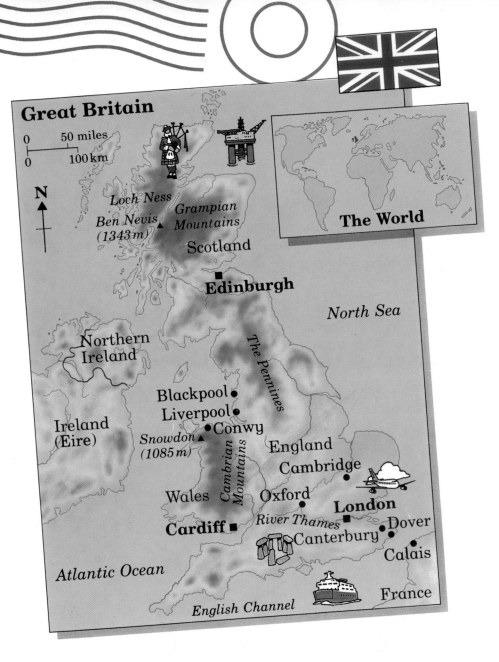

Great Britain

0 —— 50 miles
0 —— 100 km

N

Loch Ness
Ben Nevis
(1343 m)
Grampian Mountains
Scotland

Edinburgh

North Sea

Northern Ireland

The Pennines

Ireland (Eire)

Blackpool
Liverpool
Conwy
Snowdon
(1085 m)
Cambrian Mountains

England
Cambridge

Wales
Oxford
London
Cardiff
River Thames
Canterbury
Dover
Calais

Atlantic Ocean

English Channel
France

The World

A big map of Great Britain
and a small map of the world

Dear Estelle,

I am writing from England. It is part of Great Britain. You can see it marked in red on the small map. The country is quite small but about 56 million people live here.

Love,

René

P.S. Dad says that we will visit Scotland and Wales. These countries are part of Great Britain too. People in Northern Ireland are ruled from Britain, but Ireland is not part of Great Britain.

The Tower of London, England

Dear John,

We are staying in London. It is the **capital** city of England. This castle is about 1,000 years old. It is close to the River Thames. We went there on an underground train.

Love,

Will

P.S. Mum says that long ago the Tower was used as a prison. Now the Tower is a **museum**. The Crown Jewels, which the kings and queens of England wear, are kept there.

The Thames Barrier, London

Dear Rosie,

Today we went on a boat to the Thames **Barrier**. We saw new high-rise blocks and old buildings. I liked the clock tower called Big Ben the best.

Love,

Sharon

P.S. Dad says that we could not see much of the Thames Barrier because it is under the water. It can be raised to make a wall or barrier across the River Thames. This stops the river from flooding London.

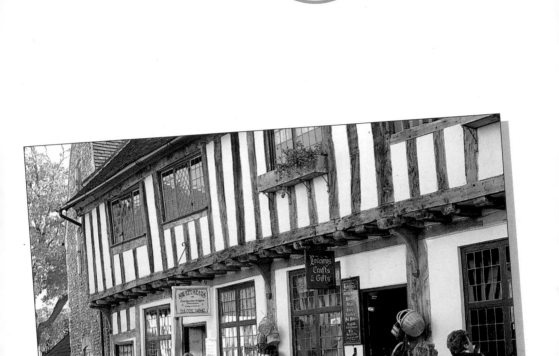

A tea shop in Lavenham, Suffolk, England

Dear Nick,

We had buns with cream and jam at this tea shop. Mum and Dad had two pots of tea! Most of the houses here are more than 400 years old.

See you soon,

Pat

P.S. Mum says that long ago Lavenham was a rich market town. People bought and sold wool here. They used some of their money to build a big church. Guess why it is called a wool church!

An Inter-City train at Euston Station, London

Dear Juliet,

We went north to Liverpool on a train like this one. My Gran lives there. There was a telephone on the train. Mum phoned Gran to say that we were on the way.

Yours,

Adam

P.S. Dad says that most people here live in towns. They like to live in houses with gardens. Many people travel by train each day to work in the cities. These people are called **commuters**.

A hovercraft from France landing at Dover, England

Dear Phil,

Dover is only 22 miles away from Calais in France. People go on day trips across the English Channel. We went on the **hovercraft**. It took about 40 minutes to get to France.

Your brother,

Andy

P.S. We saw the signs for the Channel Tunnel near Dover. The tunnel goes under the sea to France. You can travel through it on the train.

Blackpool beach, England

Dear Trasvin,

It was too cold to swim here but we went for a donkey ride. We played a game of cricket on the beach. Then we had fish and chips. Blackpool Tower is lit up at night.

Yours,

Lee

P.S. Mum says that some British families go to hot countries for their holidays. Even in the summer the sea feels cold here. It rains a lot as well! That is why the fields are so green.

Conwy Castle, Wales

Dear Erica,

We went up the highest mountain in Wales yesterday. It is called Snowdon. Today we went to see this castle. We could walk on the walls at the top. We heard people speaking Welsh in Conwy.

Your sister,

Mary

P.S. Dad says that the castle was built about 700 years ago by an English king. He built many castles in Wales.

19

Loch Ness, Scotland

Dear Ben,

There are stories or **legends** about a monster that lives in this *loch*. That is the Scottish word for a lake. Tomorrow we are going to Edinburgh. It is the capital city of Scotland.

Yours,

Colin

P.S. My friend Kirsty says she comes here every summer but she has not seen Nessie. That is the nickname for the monster. I did not see Nessie either!

The Bridge of Sighs, Cambridge, England

Dear Flora,

We came to Cambridge to see my sister Jo. She is a student here at the **university**. We went on a boat like this one. It is called a punt. Then we went to play football in the park. I love playing football!

Yours,

Mel

P.S. Mum says that most children leave school when they are 16. Some go on to study at universities such as Oxford or Cambridge.

Stonehenge, Wiltshire, England

Dear Rod,

This circle of stones is huge. It is about 3,000 years old. No one knows why the circle was built. There are stone circles in other parts of Great Britain. Stonehenge is the biggest one.

Yours,

Julian

P.S. Dad says that some people think stone circles were huge calendars. They showed the position of the Sun and the stars through the year.

Canterbury Cathedral, Kent, England

Dear Lee,

We have seen a lot of churches and **cathedrals** in Great Britain. Canterbury is an old city near Dover. Many **tourists** come to see the city and the cathedral.

Your friend,

Shirley

P.S. Mum says that Canterbury has been the the most important cathedral in England for more than 800 years. It is the world centre for **Christians** who belong to the Church of England.

27

The Union Jack flies in the
City of London

Dear Grant,

The British flag is called the Union Jack. The flag for England is white with a red cross. The flag for Scotland is blue with a white cross. The colours on the Union Jack come from these flags.

Yours,

Shane

P.S. I like the flag for Wales best. It has a red dragon on it. The Queen does not rule Great Britain now. The people choose their leaders. Great Britain is a **democracy**.

29

Glossary

Barrier: Something that keeps one thing away from another. Walls and fences are barriers.

Capital: The town or city where people who rule the country meet. It is not always the biggest city in the country.

Cathedral: The most important Christian church in an area of a country. The leader of the group of churches in the area is called a bishop.

Christian: People who follow the teachings of Jesus. Jesus lived about 2,000 years ago.

Commuter: Someone who travels some distance to and from work each day. Commuters often travel to cities to work.

Democracy: A country where all the people choose the leaders they want to run the country.

Hovercraft: A type of craft which travels over sea or land on a cushion of air.

Island: A piece of land that has water all round it.

Legend: An old story which many people believe, even though it may not be quite true.

Museum: A building where interesting things from the past are on display.

P.S.: This stands for Post Script. A postscript is the part of a card or letter which is added at the end, after the person has signed it.

Tourist: A person who is on holiday away from home.

University: A place where people go to study after they have left school.

Index